Great Hearts
Heroes of Special Olympics

Rebecca Weber

PACIFIC
LEARNING

© 2004 **Pacific Learning**
© 2004 Written by **Rebecca Weber**
Edited by **Alison Auch**
Designed by **Anna-Maria Crum**
Special thanks to Ryan Fenwick, Allison Hess, and Erin Holloway for sharing their wonderful memories and photos to make this book happen.
Additional photography: Getty Images/Stringer (p. 5); Doug Benc/Getty (p. 6)

08 07 06 05 04
10 9 8 7 6 5 4 3 2 1

Published by
Pacific Learning
P.O. Box 2723
Huntington Beach, CA 92647-0723
www.pacificlearning.com

ISBN: 978-1-59055-444-9
PL-7612

Printed in U.S.A.

Contents

Introduction

Around the world, there are more than 170 million people who have intellectual **disabilities** – 170 million! Sadly, while the world seems to be able to count the numbers, many people aren't sure what to do when they meet up with a person who lives with a mental disability.

For many years, whenever a child was born with a physical or developmental disability, doctors were likely to recommend that the child go and live in a home, and not be raised by the family.

There, children would be "warehoused," often drugged to maintain their good behavior, and without any sort of mental or physical outlet.

Luckily, over the past forty years, people have started to realize that locking away these children and adults – full of life and talent – helps nobody.

In the early 1960s, two things happened that helped change the attitudes toward intellectually disabled people. Doctors – and especially Dr. Frank Hayden of Canada – started wondering why children with intellectual disabilities were only half as physically fit as their nondisabled peers.

At about the same time, Eunice Kennedy Shriver and her husband, Sargent Shriver, were working to develop a sports program for mentally disabled people.

Eunice Kennedy Shriver plays with a mentally disabled boy.

The Shriver family

Eunice, sister to then-President John F. Kennedy, had long been interested in working with children who had special needs. She listened to the startling new evidence: If the children were helped to get in shape, they suddenly showed an amazing ability to learn new skills and participate in sports. The children who had an opportunity to exercise were happier and healthier, and progressing far beyond what anyone had ever dreamed possible.

The Shrivers' program was modest when it began in 1963. It was originally a day camp for children, held at the Shrivers' home. Five years later, they organized the first International Summer Special Olympics Games, which were held in Chicago.

At the time, nearly 1,000 athletes from the United States, Canada, and France competed.

Today, Special Olympics has grown to include more than one million athletes, who compete in 20,000 sporting events that are held in 150 countries around the world. The year-round athletic program has bettered the lives of millions of people. Here are a few of their stories.

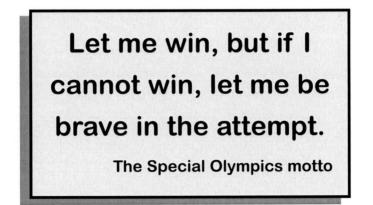

Let me win, but if I cannot win, let me be brave in the attempt.

The Special Olympics motto

Ryan's Story

CHAPTER

A Promise Kept

"Hey, bro, can you give us some push-ups?"

Without hesitation, fifteen-year-old Ryan Fenwick flashes a smile at his mom, and drops to the ground. With arm muscles swelling, he counts off the push-ups ten at a time – he doesn't seem to get tired even as the numbers climb.

Around him, Ryan's walls are filled with medals, trophies, and photographs of famous athletes. A closer look shows that Ryan is in most of the photos, right next to the megastars of the sports world.

This is fitting, because Ryan is an exceptional athlete too.

Fifteen years before, when Ryan's parents learned he had been born with **Down syndrome** (DS), they made themselves a promise: No matter what, Ryan would have every chance they could possibly give him.

Today, that promise has more than been fulfilled.

Ryan, who is home-schooled because of his incredibly busy athletic schedule, trains for and competes in more than ten different sports a year.

Of all the sports, his favorites are ice hockey and basketball. No matter what the weather is like, he is outside practicing every day of the year. He is determined to be the best player, out on the ice or on the court. His motto: "I like to win. I *want* to win!"

Still, winning is only part of what Ryan is working for. To really understand him, it's important to know how it all began. As a baby and toddler, Ryan faced severe delays in his development. He couldn't sit up. He couldn't walk. When he was three years old, his parents had to carry him everywhere.

Every milestone was a challenge. Every small achievement was a huge victory – a cause for celebration. Little by little, Ryan and his parents worked to help him meet physical goals that come easily and naturally to other children.

CHAPTER 1

Ryan learns skating tricks from Rob Blake, a professional hockey player.

Children with Down syndrome often face these kinds of struggles. For the most part, they are usually smaller than their **peers**, and their physical and mental development are slower.

While other children usually walk between twelve and fourteen months of age, children with DS often don't walk until they are three years old. This is because

Swimming helped Ryan build strength and coordination.

> **Facts about
> Down Syndrome:**
>
> • the rate of Down syndrome births is
>   between 1 in 1,000 and 1 in 1,100
> • each year, approximately 3,000—5,000
>   children are born with this chromosomal
>   disorder.

children with DS face physical challenges that range from decreased muscle tone to skeletal problems and loose **ligaments**. Many also have bad eyesight, and small hands and feet.

Still, Ryan and his family refused to give up. They struggled together. After a while, they started to see results. Big results.

By the time he was five years old, Ryan had progressed to the point where he could start playing soccer.

This turned out to be the best physical outlet for his tireless energy. When Ryan could get exercise – and lots of it – life was good, and he did really well. Everything started to fall into place.

By the time he was eight, Ryan branched into ice hockey, which has since become his favorite sport. He'll gladly play any position, although his favorites are defense, and of course any position that will allow him to score.

Then, when Ryan was nine, he became involved in Special Olympics. Almost immediately, he was in year-round training to compete in an entirely new set of sports. While several months of the year were still devoted to his ice-hockey league, Ryan filled in every other available moment with seasonal Special Olympics sports.

He started in track and field. Then he progressed to swimming. By 2000, he had added softball, golf, basketball, skiing, swimming, floor hockey, and volleyball to his roster.

Soon, Ryan's entire family was involved in his whirlwind schedule. While he practices

and competes with other athletes, Ryan's mom, dad, and sister have been able to meet other families with special needs children. Strong friendships formed, both on and off the field.

CHAPTER

A Full Calendar

Ryan's year revolves around his sports schedule. Aside from ice hockey and soccer, every sport he plays is organized by Special Olympics.

Winter Schedule — January to March

During the winter months, Ryan competes in ice hockey, skiing, swimming, and basketball.

Every Saturday, he and his dad get up at 4:30 in the morning and head for the mountains. There, Ryan skis for the entire day, practicing his racing moves and learning new strategies.

On Sunday, Ryan has an hour of hockey practice, and from there goes straight to swimming practice.

Basketball practice falls on Wednesday night, and every other day of the week, Ryan alternates between hockey and basketball practice at his home.

The hard work has paid off. An excellent hockey player, Ryan has come close to scoring the ultimate hockey dream – a **hat trick** – two separate times.

In skiing, Ryan is also making a name for himself. Each season, Ryan gets a chance to compete against other athletes at local area meets. If he skis well, he qualifies for the state competitions. In the past two years, he has won gold medals for his skiing at the state tournament. His scores were so strong, he almost qualified to ski at the International Games that were held in Nagano, Japan.

When Ryan first started swimming, he needed a little help. Not anymore!

Spring Schedule — April to June

As the weather warms up, Ryan moves into a whole new realm of sports. Literally, Ryan and his family start running – to practice and for practice.

The weekends pass like a blur. Every Saturday Ryan has an hour and a half of soccer practice, which is immediately followed by two hours of track. Sundays, he trains for a national ice-hockey tournament, and then goes to swimming practice.

In the middle of the week, there are yet more track practices. Ryan's best event is the 100 meter, although he also excels at the long jump and relay races.

Summer Schedule — July to September

The hot summer months are the only time of the year that Ryan isn't working on his

hockey skills. During his time off the ice, he instead fills his days training for golf and softball.

In golf, Ryan works on both team play and his individual golfing skills. Softball is also all about the team – Ryan's strong competitive streak works well in these sports. He wants to win, and he's happy to do whatever he can to help his team get ahead.

The summer wraps up with a huge golf tournament held at a local course.

Fall Schedule — September to December

For Ryan, crisp autumn Saturdays are dominated by soccer. Intense ice-hockey practices begin again each Sunday, followed by swimming. This is also the season for floor hockey and volleyball. Ryan fits in practice times whenever he can during the week.

Despite his killer schedule, Ryan never seems to tire. In fact, the more he does, the happier he is.

3

The Fame Game

Even though Ryan's life seems filled with the sporting side of Special Olympics, the organization has done much more for him and for his family.

One of the biggest perks is the events Ryan gets to attend. Every year, Special Olympics chooses an athlete to help out at an NHL game.

In 2003, Ryan was chosen to be the "Stick Kid" for the Colorado Avalanche's first preseason game. In addition to getting the best seat in the house to watch the game, Ryan got to meet his hero, Joe Sakic, captain of the Avalanche.

Ryan, his friend Matt, and sister Kristen at an NHL game.

Big names are also involved with the Special Olympics sports. Scott Weaver, the president of Colorado Special Olympics, coaches Ryan's floor-hockey and volleyball teams for three hours every Monday night.

At the "Hoop It Up" Special Olympics basketball clinic, players from Denver's NBA team, the Nuggets, worked with Ryan and other players to hone their skills. As a special bonus, the Denver Nuggets then gave all of the clinic participants free tickets to see a professional game.

On top of everything else, Ryan has been the star of a television commercial with the Colorado Rockies baseball team, and has also been featured on a popular morning radio show.

Ryan, during his radio interview

*Ryan and two of his Unified Partners,
Matt and Kristen*

As much as Ryan has enjoyed meeting
famous athletes, some of his best memories
are the times he's been able to compete
with his friend Matt, who has been Ryan's
Unified Partner for several different sports.

A Unified Partner is a nondisabled peer
(sometimes an adult, sometimes a
teenager) who takes part in the sports
along with the Special Olympics athletes.

In 2003 and 2004, Matt and Ryan skied
as a Unified Team and won medal after
medal in the downhill races at the area

Ryan and Matt, after a successful run

meets, and then in the state meet. Their best scores were in Giant Slalom in 2003. In softball, Matt has been the pitcher for Ryan's team, and helps train the athletes in skills and strategies to win.

Ryan's sister, Kristen, has also been a Unified Partner for some of Ryan's sports. It's a great way for the athletes to form lifelong friendships with people outside of the Special Olympics organization.

From the very first days of his life, Ryan has fought to get ahead. He and his family worked together to help him learn to walk and talk.

Today, they work together as his athletic skills carry him into increasingly prestigious international competitions.

Ryan's mom, Lori, believes that Special Olympics makes this sort of dream possible for many people. It pays for the athlete's expenses, so that families don't have to worry about finding the money for their children to participate. It allows possibilities and creates dreams where there may have been none.

In the past, it was considered normal for children who had Down syndrome to lead **sedentary** lives. Many suffered from heart problems, which were compounded by weight problems.

Ryan, deep into his push-ups, shows that there is another way.

Allison's Story

CHAPTER

Life at Its Fullest

"Whew – that week is going to be tough. I have something planned for every day. On Friday, I have to be out of the house by four because I'm going to be a deejay for a dance that night."

At twenty-four years old, Allison Hess is a woman on the move. She works as a deejay, she holds down a volunteer job with the

Department of Motor Vehicles, and she competes in as many Special Olympic sports as she possibly can fit into her busy schedule.

Although swimming is Allison's favorite sport, she also competes in bowling, skiing, softball, and basketball.

Even more important to Allison is the work she does for Special Olympics as one of its Global Messengers. When she is wearing her Global Messenger hat, Allison travels around to teach people about

Special Olympics, and to raise funds for the **nonprofit**. In her speeches to large corporations, Allison shares what Special Olympics has meant to her.

Watching Allison up in front of a large audience, it is hard to imagine the challenges she has overcome to get there.

When Allison was born, she didn't get enough oxygen, which caused brain damage that resulted in **cerebral palsy**. This is the name for a group of chronic conditions that can affect a body's ability to move and control its muscles.

Facts about Cerebral Palsy:

- 765,000 children and adults in the United States have some form of cerebral palsy
- each year, about 8,000 infants are diagnosed with the condition

Like most young children with cerebral palsy, Allison had difficulty crawling and walking. She also faced learning challenges and **epilepsy**.

However, Allison was always positive and determined. From her very youngest days, she struggled to make and achieve goals. Her friends and family members recognized what a special person Allison was from the start.

Allison didn't just want to help herself. The truth is, she wanted to help everybody else too.

In 1985, when she was only five years old, Allison was a poster child for United Way. Her poster, titled "Success Story," outlined both her struggles and successes. Allison's story did a great deal to raise the

public's awareness about living with a disability in today's world.

Allison's time in the spotlight didn't end there. In 1990, she modeled for a local department store and appeared in their newspaper advertisements. A year later, when she was only eleven years old, Allison was invited to speak at a workshop in front of more than 100 teachers.

By sharing her triumphs and struggles with these teachers, she helped them better understand how they could help special needs students in their classrooms.

As she helped others, Allison worked hard to make her own life as full as possible. She was active in her school choir from third grade through her senior year in high school. She took dance lessons and starred in recitals. She challenged herself to get ahead in school.

Still, something seemed to be missing. Then, when she was a junior in high school, Allison saw fliers for Special Olympics in her school. She didn't know anything about the program, but it looked like a great chance to get involved with something new, and to meet new people.

CHAPTER

A New Commitment

Allison's mom and dad contacted a local representative for Special Olympics, and within days, Allison had started bowling and skiing with a new coach. The more she competed, the more she enjoyed herself, and soon she was signing up for every other sport that interested her.

Allison quickly learned that she not only enjoyed competing – she was good at it! Even though many of the people she was competing against had been part of Special Olympics since they were eight years old, Allison soon caught on to the rules. The ribbons and trophies started to pile up.

Suddenly Allison, who had always been fairly active, was hardly ever at home. In the autumn, her time is taken up with bowling practice and competitions. In the winter, it's all about skiing and basketball. From February to June, Allison practices her swimming at a local high school, and competes in area and state meets. Summers are fully taken up with softball.

On days off, and she doesn't get many, Allison walks her dog so that they can both stay in good shape. This is especially important when she isn't swimming regularly, such as during basketball and softball seasons.

Allison, who competes in all her chosen sports, has won at the state level several times. Occasionally, she finds herself competing against up to 100 other athletes.

There is no age limit, and many of the older competitors have done a great deal to help Allison. They have also served as an inspiration to her – if they can compete into their seventies and eighties, so can she.

In her own way, Allison was also singled out to be an inspiration to others. Her positive and helpful spirit caught the notice of people who work for Special Olympics. In 2001, she was asked if she wanted to become a Global Messenger, and she jumped at the chance.

CHAPTER 5

To get started, Allison and a few other Colorado athletes went to a three-day training seminar. They had to do a lot of homework and some on-the-spot training. The Global Messengers were filmed and evaluated, to make sure they would be able to handle the pressure of live presentations in front of unfamiliar audiences.

None of this worried Allison for a minute. Presenting in front of a hundred or more people? In her own words, it was a piece of cake!

Helping Others to Help

Now that she has worked as a Global Messenger for a few years, Allison knows exactly what to do whenever she is scheduled to speak somewhere – something that happens at least one or two times every month.

As soon as she knows her next speaking date, Allison works with her father, whom she calls her official speechwriter. Together, they prepare whatever she needs to say to suit the occasion.

Then the practices start. Allison practices each new speech as many times as she can, so that she knows it cold. Even though she

always has the words in front of her, she enjoys looking out at the audience as she speaks, and she doesn't want to worry about losing her place.

Then she and her dad hit the road so that she can give her usual polished presentation.

As a Global Messenger, Allison doesn't just raise people's awareness about Special Olympics. With poise and style, she shows the positive impact it can have on the lives of people who have forgotten how to hope.

Allison – who isn't paid a cent for her work as a Global Messenger – has raised countless dollars for Special Olympics, both in corporate and personal donations.

This money is critically important. Special Olympics depends entirely on donations to support the programs and to allow the athletes to get to and compete in any sports they want, completely free of charge.

This is part of the reason Allison is happy to work so hard. Besides attending events such as golf tournaments and corporate retreats, Allison's duties as a Global Messenger have put her in contact with powerful politicians, which helps raise awareness even further.

On May 30, 2002, Allison was invited to speak with Colorado's governor, from the steps of the Colorado state capital building. Allison gave a speech that honored law enforcement officers in order to kick off the summer's "Torch Run" – a major Special Olympics fund-raiser.

In 2003, Governor Bill Owens and Allison spoke together again, this time on television, working together to raise money and awareness about Special Olympics.

Many people have found ways to thank Allison for her hard work and dedication. In addition to inducting her into the National Honor Society, her old high school honored her work in Special Olympics with a special ceremony and two standing ovations.

A local television station has even featured Allison in a special-interest segment during an evening newscast.

Best of all, Allison won the 2000 Special Olympics Colorado "Outstanding Female Athlete of the Year" award.

Allison and Colorado Governor Bill Owens

As she was inducted into the Special Olympics Hall of Fame, Special Olympics made sure this was a night to remember for Allison. Surrounded by local and national celebrities, Allison gave a speech that brought her family and her boyfriend, Michael, to tears.

Although 2004 is Allison's last year of working as a Global Messenger, she plans to continue her work helping others.

Volunteer work has been one of Allison's top priorities ever since she was thirteen.

Her first volunteer job was at a charitable food program, where she worked in a food warehouse to help the hungry.

In 1995, Allison started volunteering at Bal Swan's Children's Center – a preschool that is designed around the special needs of disabled children, as well as more typical children. Allison attended Bal Swan's when she was younger, and wanted to give back to

Allison and former football star
Joe Namath at her induction into
the Hall of Fame

a place that had helped her immensely with her physical and educational needs. Allison has even volunteered at a local elementary school, working with students.

Lately, Allison has turned her boundless energy to a new cause. On the first Friday of each month, she and her father have organized a special dance.

This dance, which is held at a local church, is specifically for people who live with physical and intellectual disabilities.

Allison and her dad share the disc jockey duties, and with each event, Allison is taking more and more of a lead in choosing the music and setting the pace of the dance.

As always, when Allison is involved, she knows how to focus attention on her cause. Even though the idea for the dances is still new, Allison has already been interviewed by a local news station about the whole concept behind the dances. With the attention, the number of attendees is growing.

Allison, deejay extraordinaire!

Pulling together something like this would be an achievement for anybody. For Allison, it's just another small way to repay the people who have done so much for her. In her own life, Allison feels that she has everything she's ever wanted. Now she wants to make this same happiness a reality for people who might be struggling.

As for Special Olympics, Allison will be there for as long as she's able. After all, as she herself has said in one of her speeches, "Special Olympics is not about who wins or loses. It's about the chance to touch the ball."

Erin's Story

CHAPTER

7

How to Rise Above

"Life wasn't very good back then," Erin says, her eyes focused more on the past than on the beautiful farmland around her. She is broken out of her reverie by the gentle nudge of a horse – her horse, the horse she raised and trained.

Erin had just been describing her childhood, and many of her memories were painful. When she was in her teens, Erin stopped going to school and started working in her mom's pet-grooming business. She always felt comfortable when she was working with animals. She did a good job in her work, but she always knew she was capable of doing much more.

Erin's mother didn't think that Erin would every be able to hold a job, or do any

real work. She didn't think Erin could even take care of herself. Eventually, Erin's mother – following the advice of workers at the state Social Services department – placed Erin in a group home.

This home, which was geared toward people who had mental illnesses, was a dreary place for Erin. Even though she was only in her early twenties, Erin's days were lost in the haze of the medications she was given to keep her calm and quiet.

Erin lived in the group home for almost three years. She had very little freedom, and even less money available to her, but somehow, she still found a way out.

Erin received $1.50 each weekday, and $1.25 each weekend day. Even though most of this money was stolen from her by some of the violent patients who lived in the home, Erin always managed to hide away enough for weekly escapes.

Every Saturday, Erin and her friends would take the bus downtown so that they could play sports together. Even if Erin only had enough money to pay her bus fare that week, the excursions gave her hope.

It was during these dark days that Erin became involved in Special Olympics.

How her life was about to change!

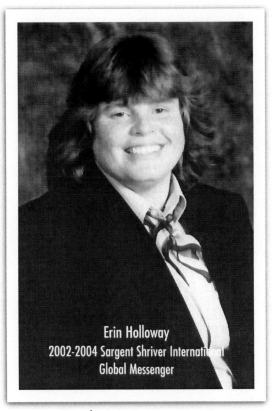

Erin Holloway
2002-2004 Sargent Shriver International
Global Messenger

Erin's business card

For the first time in her life, Erin started to hear praise. After one of her first swimming practices, a coach told her that she had done a great job.

The next four years passed like a blur. Erin was swimming twice a week with Special Olympics – thousands of laps – and finding herself.

She began to make new friends. Slowly, she found that she was able to trust people, and then she began to trust herself.

With each day that went by, Erin gained skills and independence. She was able to move out of the despised group home and get an apartment.

Her new friends helped her stop taking the medication that had so dulled her life. Together, they flushed it down the toilet.

The team sports she was playing taught her how to work with other people. For the first time in her life, she was surrounded by people that she could depend on, and they all were working to achieve something together.

Before she knew it, Erin – the woman who was never expected to work or care for herself – was working more than sixty hours a week, at two different jobs.

Giving Back

Today, twenty-four years after she first became a part of Special Olympics, Erin has become an amazing success story.

A talented athlete, Erin has won more than 100 medals over the years, competing in sixteen different sports. Some of her greatest success was in power lifting. She qualified for the national games that year, which were held in San Antonio, Texas. There, up against the top six power lifters in the country, Erin won a bronze medal.

She still trains for and competes in Alpine skiing, golf, basketball, softball, floor hockey, and soccer. However, she has taken her years of experience and found ways to help the organization that gave her back her life.

In 1997, Erin underwent rigorous U.S. Skiing Federation training so that she could become an Alpine Racing Official for Special Olympics.

As a race official, she has traveled to games nationally and internationally, and her goal wherever she goes is to watch over beginning skiers. She works to make sure that each athlete goes home both safe and happy.

Before Special Olympics had even created their Global Messenger positions, people started asking Erin to share her experiences. A 1989 Hall of Fame inductee herself, Erin started speaking at the ceremonies to recognize new athletes.

In 1998, she was invited to go to the White House for the thirtieth anniversary of Special Olympics. There, she was introduced to President Bill Clinton. At every turn, she met another celebrity. The

Erin meets President Clinton

Shriver family was there, as were countless other actors, singers, and athletes.

Every single person who heard her story was stunned – Erin was quickly making a name for herself as someone who could get and keep people's attention.

When Special Olympics decided to create the Global Messenger positions, Erin was a natural choice. She flew to Los Angeles for training, and within a few days was ready to start. Her graduation assignment was tough, for she had to give a speech in front of Sargent and Eunice Kennedy Shriver, the very people who had helped found Special Olympics in the first place, back in the 1960s.

Jack Hess (Special Olympics Canada), Tim Shriver, and Erin

After her speech, Erin got to go and celebrate. Before she knew it, she found herself walking down the red carpet at the rerelease of the movie *ET.* She met Steven Spielberg and Drew Barrymore, and went to the huge celebrity-packed party afterward. At that moment, she could barely even remember what her life had been like in the bad old days.

CHAPTER

Going International

In 2002, Erin's work as a Global Messenger changed dramatically. To honor Sargent Shriver for his work, Special Olympics created an elite team of International Global Messengers who travel to events around the world.

Special Olympics has called its International Global Messengers the "leaders and message-bearers of the movement." Out of the ninety people who were nominated, Erin was one of twelve athletes from around the world chosen for this honored position. Together, these International Global Messengers set out to

share the Special Olympics ideals of hope, acceptance, dignity, and courage with people all over the world.

Erin started to rack up frequent flier miles with all of the trips that followed this appointment. She has traveled to Toronto in Canada, Peru in South America, and the Special Olympics Summer World Games that were held in Ireland in 2003.

These games were the largest sporting event in the world that year. More than

7,000 different athletes from 150 different countries were there to compete. Erin had never had a bigger audience for her message.

While she was in Ireland, she gave presentations in Dublin and Belfast. As always, her story of triumph over adversity captivated the audiences.

Erin's willingness to share painful memories was powerful in two different

Erin and ex-boxer Mohammed Ali

ways. It offered a message of pure hope to her fellow athletes. It also helped "typical" people understand what life could be like for people who have intellectual or physical disabilities.

"The first feeling I look back on was the feeling of shame," Erin always explains at the start of her speeches. "I felt this shame one day at school, when the other kids started to believe that I was different. They believed that it was okay to make fun of me, and to call me names."

Day by day, as she was left to sit alone, rejected by others, Erin became more and more introverted. She tried to hide, even when sitting in plain sight. Her hair grew shaggy, covering her eyes so that people couldn't see how they hurt her. She stopped speaking so she could avoid the labels "stupid" and "retarded."

Whenever Erin finishes one of her speeches, she always looks out over the audience, watching their reactions. She is never disappointed. The girl who once refused to talk, has become a woman who is now one of Special Olympics' primary spokespeople, both nationally and internationally.

Once a Global Messenger, Always a Global Messenger

Erin's term as an International Global Messenger is set to expire at the end of 2004. Still, she plans to continue to use her skills to help Special Olympics.

One thing she is going to do is continue to help raise money. With her international reputation as a gifted speaker, Erin has worked as a keynote speaker at several different fund-raisers. In August 2003, she participated in an event that raised more than two million dollars for Special Olympics.

In recent years, Erin has also discovered that she is interested in politics, both within Special Olympics and in a much broader sense.

She has served on the board of Special Olympics Colorado for six years, where she refuses to sit back and let decisions be made around her.

She went into her term on the board with a mission: she was going to work to help current and future board members feel comfortable and accepted – especially if they were coming to the board as athletes.

She was also determined to make sure that the athletes would have a chance to participate both fully and meaningfully in any decisions the board might make.

In addition, Erin used her public speaking skills when she addressed the Colorado State Legislature on three different occasions. Her persuasive dialogue helped convince these jaded politicians to give Colorado Special

Olympics an amazing fund-raising tool. Today, thanks in part to Erin's efforts, Colorado taxpayers can make an instant donation simply by checking a box on their yearly tax form.

Erin's role with Special Olympics has changed dramatically since those first days when she had to hide bus fare just to get to the swimming pool.

Today, when she is not off on speaking engagements or working at either of her

two jobs, she works on the ranch that she and her roommate own outside of the city. She raises and trains horses, and rescues any abused or tormented animal that may cross her path.

Erin feels just as strongly about the need to help and protect people. As new athletes enter the program, Erin is there to make sure they succeed beyond even their own dreams. New Global Messengers? Erin is there to help them with their speeches.

To her, Special Olympics is family. They were there for her when no one else was, and now it is her turn to work for them. When she thinks about it, all she can do is smile. "Special Olympics won't get rid of me. As long as I can move, I'll be doing something."

To Get Involved

If you want to become part of the Special Olympics team, there are many ways you can help create success stories such as Ryan's, Allison's, and Erin's.

Coaches

If you love a particular sport, think about sharing some of your time to teach this sport to others. As a coach, you would become a role model, and help build the confidence and character of the most courageous and enthusiastic group of athletes you'll ever meet. All that is required is two to four hours a week.

Unified Partners

Do you want to get out there and play too? Think about becoming a Unified Partner – you'll not only be able to take part, you'll know that, with your help, the athletes will achieve sports glory they never dreamed of.

Support Crew

For Special Olympics to function, it needs thousands of volunteers to do every duty from timing events to helping organize a state competition. Your time and energy can help so much.

For more information about how you can become a part of the amazing Special Olympics success story, go to:

www.specialolympics.org

The Special Olympics Code of Conduct Sportsmanship

- I will practice good sportsmanship.
- I will act in ways that bring respect to me, my coaches, my team and Special Olympics.
- I will not use bad language.
- I will not swear or insult other persons.
- I will not fight with other athletes, coaches, volunteers or staff.

Index

Glossary

cerebral palsy – a disability resulting from brain damage that happens during or shortly after a birth in which a baby does not get enough oxygen

disability – a mental or physical condition that makes someone different from "typical" people

Down syndrome – a condition that a person is born with, which can affect physical and intellectual development

epilepsy – a disorder that affects the brain, causing convulsions and loss of consciousness

hat trick – when a single player scores three goals during one sports game

ligament – a band of tough tissue in the body that connects bone or cartilage, or holds organs in place

nonprofit – an organization whose goal is not to make a profit, but rather to make enough money to keep running. Many nonprofits are dedicated to helping others.

peer – a person who belongs to the same age group as another person

sedentary – describes a lifestyle that involves little to no physical activity

80